THANK YOU SO MUCH!
I REALLY APPRECIATE IT.

SPEAK THEIR LANGUAGE!

HAVE YOU EVER NOTICED THAT WHEN YOUR PARENTS DEMAND SOMETHING FROM YOU, OR WHEN THEY WANT YOU TO UNDERSTAND SOME IMPORTANT THING, THEY USE BIG LONG WORDS? I AM A PARENT TOO, SO I CAN TELL YOU, ALL PARENTS DO THIS. WHEN GROWNUPS GET SERIOUS OR WORRIED, THEY USE SERIOUS GROWNUP LANGUAGE, WHICH MEANS **BIG WORDS.**

WELL, I THINK **IT'S TIME KIDS LEARN SOME BIG WORDS** TO RESPOND TO THEIR PARENTS IN A WAY THAT IMPRESSES THEM. SOME PARENTS MAY BE SO SURPRISED TO HEAR YOU SPEAK THEIR LANGUAGE, THEY WILL JUST ROLL BELLY UP (WHICH MEANS *GIVE UP*) AND DO WHATEVER YOU ASK.

I THINK IT'S POSSIBLE.

WHEN MY SON TALKS TO ME IN A GROWNUP WAY, I MELT LIKE ICE ON A HOT SUMMER DAY, AND CHASE THAT ICE CREAM TRUCK TO BUY HIM 3 CHOCOLATE ICE CREAMS, EVEN THOUGH I KNOW HE WILL EAT ONLY ONE, AND THE REST WILL DRIP ALL OVER MY FANCY SHOES.

WHEN THEY USE BIG WORDS

BIG WORDS OFTEN MEAN SOMEONE IS MAD AT YOU.
FOR EXAMPLE, WHEN YOU HEAR
THE WORD **CONSEQUENCES** AS IN:
THERE WILL BE CONSEQUENCES!
YOU KNOW THAT TROUBLE IS NEAR.

AND IF YOU HEAR THE WORD
RAMIFICATIONS
ANOTHER WORD FOR BAD CONSEQUENCES,
AS IN **RAMIFICATIONS OF YOUR BEHAVIOR**,
RUN! A REAL DISASTER IS COMING!

...RAMIFICATIONS OF YOUR BEHAVIOR!

ON THE OTHER HAND, LONG WORDS ARE OFTEN USED
TO PRAISE YOU. IF, INSTEAD OF SAYING *GOOD* OR *GREAT*,
A GROWNUP SAYS YOUR DECISION
OR YOUR WORK IS
BRILLIANT, OR
WOO-HOO!
YOU HAVE
WOWED THEM!

SPECTACULAR

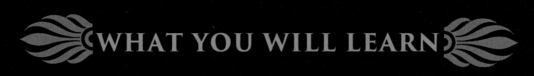
WHAT YOU WILL LEARN

PARENTS SO WANT THEIR KIDS TO BE RESPONSIBLE AND
SERIOUS, THEY WILL DO ANYTHING, EVEN BUY YOU THIS BOOK,
TO TEACH YOU **HOW TO BEAT THEM AT THEIR OWN
BIG WORDS GAME**! IN THIS BOOK I WILL SHARE WITH YOU
SECRET TRICKS AND WORDS TO IMPRESS GROWNUPS,
AS WELL AS **THE STRATEGY** (BIG WORD FOR **PLAN**)
TO **REQUEST** (BIG WORD FOR **ASK**) WHAT YOU WANT
IN A WAY THAT IS **IRRESISTIBLE**
(BIG WORD FOR: **THEY CAN'T SAY NO TO YOU**).

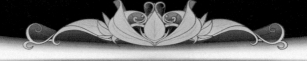

FIRST WE'LL LEARN **DIPLOMAT'S ENGLISH**.
IT MAKES GROWNUPS LISTEN TO YOU.
NEXT WE'LL LEARN **PROFESSOR'S ENGLISH**.
IT MAKES YOU SOUND BRILLIANT, SO GROWNUPS
TAKE YOUR IDEAS SERIOUSLY.
THINK OF PROFESSORS' ENGLISH AS
A CAKE MADE OF BIG WORDS WITH
SOME FRENCH AND LATIN SAYINGS FOR ICING.
AND FINALLY WE'LL MASTER THE MAGIC OF
GETTING TO YES
WHEN YOU NEED SOMETHING FROM A GROWNUP.

*OK, BEFORE YOUR PARENTS REALIZE WHAT THIS BOOK
IS REALLY ABOUT, LET'S GET RIGHT DOWN TO BUSINESS AND
LEARN WHERE OUR BIG WORDS COME FROM!*

THE NORMAN CONQUEST

CONQUEST IS A WAR VICTORY, WHERE THE WINNERS TAKE OVER THE COUNTRY THEY DEFEATED.

IN 1066 WILLIAM THE CONQUEROR (WHO CAME FROM NORMANDY IN THE NORTH OF FRANCE) DEFEATED ENGLAND IN A BATTLE AND BECAME THE ENGLISH KING.

HE GAVE HIS FRENCH FRIENDS FROM NORMANDY ALL THE JOBS IN THE GOVERNMENT AND THE ARMY, AND THE ENGLISH HAD TO LEARN A LOT OF FRENCH TO TALK TO THEIR NEW NORMAN LEADERS.

THE OLD ENGLISH LANGUAGE WAS NOW ONLY FOR PEOPLE IN THE COUNTRYSIDE. TO BE SUCCESSFUL YOU HAD TO MIX FRENCH WORDS INTO YOUR ENGLISH. AND AT THE ROYAL COURT THEY SPOKE ONLY FRENCH!

WELL, GUESS WHAT: A LOT OF THE BIG WORDS YOUR PARENTS USE ARE THOSE FRENCH WORDS FROM NORMANDY! SO WHEN YOU TALK TO YOUR PARENTS, IMAGINE YOU ARE TALKING TO WILLIAM THE CONQUEROR AND USE THE WORDS HE WOULD UNDERSTAND AND LIKE!

GERMANIC AND LATIN WORDS

INSTEAD OF COOL SAY **SPECTACULAR,**
INSTEAD OF PRETTY SAY **EXQUISITE,**
INSTEAD OF GREAT SAY **MARVELOUS.**

IF WILLIAM THE CONQUEROR HEARD
YOU SPEAK LIKE THIS, HE WOULD
GIVE YOU HALF HIS KINGDOM!

ENGLISH IS A GERMANIC LANGUAGE.
IT COMES FROM ANCIENT LANGUAGES OF NORTHERN EUROPE
THAT WERE SPOKEN BY GERMANIC TRIBES.
OLD ENGLISH (GERMANIC) WORDS ARE USUALLY SHORT.
THE FRENCH LANGUAGE COMES
MOSTLY FROM LATIN,
AND WORDS OF LATIN ORIGIN
ARE **LONGER.**
LATIN WAS SPOKEN
IN ANCIENT ROME, AND LATER
BECAME THE LANGUAGE USED IN
LAW, SCIENCE, AND CHURCH BOOKS.
IN MODERN ENGLISH MOST
FANCY BIG WORDS ARE
FRENCH-LATIN WORDS.

BY THE WAY, AFTER WILLIAM THE CONQUEROR
BECAME THE ENGLISH KING, PARENTS STARTED GIVING
KIDS HIS NAME IN ENGLAND. BEFORE THAT
WILLIAM WAS A FRENCH NAME, EVEN THOUGH
IT IS MADE OF 2 GERMANIC WORDS:
WILL = WISH
HELM = PROTECTION (SAME AS IN THE WORD *HELMET*).

A GHOST STORY

Here is the same story written with
1. short Germanic words, and
2. long French-Latin words.

Notice that the second version is **longer** than the first, because we are using big words!

1. I came home and saw a strange thing: The light at my place was on. Anyone here? I asked, very surprised. At first I guessed, maybe it was a ghost. But that idea seemed funny. It just made no sense. Then I thought the light switch is broken, and I didn't know. I was worried and afraid. Then my mom called and told me she had brought me a cake and left it in the kitchen.

2. I arrived at my residence and observed a bizzarre phenomenon: My domicile was illuminated. Anyone present? I inquired, exceedingly perplexed. Initially, I surmised it was, conceivably, an apparition. But that hypothesis appeared ridiculous. It was just preposterous. Consequently, I speculated the light switch had malfunctioned, and I hadn't discerned that. I felt distressed and apprehensive. Then my mom telephoned and informed me she had delivered a cake for me and deposited it in the kitchen.

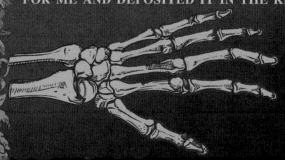

HAROLD   BATTLE

HAROLD HIT BY AN ARROW

DIPLOMATS

DIPLOMATS ARE PEOPLE SENT BY THE GOVERNMENT OF ONE COUNTRY TO ANOTHER COUNTRY TO HELP THE TWO COUNTRIES UNDERSTAND EACH OTHER AND BE FRIENDS.

IF THE TWO COUNTRIES NEED TO AGREE ON SOMETHING, LIKE WHETHER PEOPLE NEED A **VISA** (PERMISSION) TO TRAVEL ACROSS THE BORDER, OR HOW THESE COUNTRIES **TRADE** (BUY OR SELL THINGS TO EACH OTHER), DIPLOMATS WORK OUT THE AGREEMENTS (CALLED **TREATIES**) THROUGH **NEGOTIATIONS** (OR TALKS).

DIPLOMATS MUST BE **DIPLOMATIC**, THAT IS VERY CAREFUL IN WHAT THEY SAY AND HOW THEY SAY THINGS, BECAUSE IF THEY MAKE A MISTAKE IT CAN RESULT IN BAD RELATIONS BETWEEN THE COUNTRIES OR EVEN IN A WAR!

2 DIPLOMATS SHAKING HANDS

PEOPLE MAKE FUN OF DIPLOMATS FOR BEING ALWAYS SO CAREFUL AND THINKING SO HARD BEFORE SAYING ANYTHING.

HERE ARE A COUPLE 1-LINE JOKES ABOUT DIPLOMATS:

- **A DIPLOMAT THINKS TWICE BEFORE SAYING NOTHING.**
- **A DIPLOMAT KNOWS HOW FAR TO GO BEFORE HE GOES TOO FAR.**

DIPLOMATS WIN!

IF WE ALL WERE AS CAREFUL
AS DIPLOMATS WHEN WE SPEAK,
WE WOULD NEVER GET INTO
TROUBLE, AND WE WOULD
ALWAYS WIN IN ARGUMENTS
AND NEGOTIATIONS.

BEING A DIPLOMAT IS **A GOOD CAREER,** TOO -
LOTS OF TRAVEL AND SPEAKING FOREIGN LANGUAGES.

DIPLOMATS ALSO HAVE TO BE
EXTREMELY (BIG WORD FOR *VERY*) **POLITE**
AND **FRIENDLY,** BECAUSE POLITENESS AND
FRIENDLINESS GET PEOPLE TO SAY **YES** TO YOU.
AND THAT'S WHAT YOU WANT AS A DIPLOMAT.
YOU WANT PEOPLE TO ALWAYS SAY **YES** TO YOU
SO YOU CAN NEGOTIATE THE BEST TREATY
FOR YOUR COUNTRY.

IF YOU ARE DIPLOMATIC LIKE A DIPLOMAT,
GROWNUPS WILL ALWAYS LISTEN TO YOU AND
WILL TAKE SERIOUSLY WHAT YOU ARE TELLING THEM.
IF YOU ARE SAYING SOMETHING
THEY DON'T WANT TO HEAR, BUT YOU SAY IT
DIPLOMATICALLY, THEY WON'T BE UPSET!

EVERY DIPLOMAT KNOWS WHAT MATTERS:
IT'S NOT WHAT YOU SAY. IT'S HOW YOU SAY IT!

SO LET'S LEARN HOW DIPLOMATS TALK.

PLEASE IS NOT ENOUGH.

DIPLOMATS ARE SUPER POLITE, BECAUSE
THEY WANT PEOPLE TO RESPECT AND LIKE THEM,
SO WHEN THE TIME COMES TO ASK FOR SOMETHING,
PEOPLE WILL SAY **YES** TO A SUPER NICE DIPLOMAT.

WE ALL KNOW HOW TO USE THE MAGIC WORD *PLEASE*,
BUT IF YOU ARE A DIPLOMAT, *PLEASE* IS NOT ENOUGH.

HERE IS HOW TO ASK FOR SOMETHING
LIKE A DIPLOMAT.

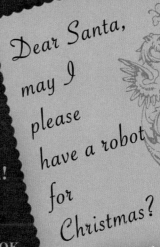

Dear Santa, may I please have a robot for Christmas?

DON'T SAY: I WANT A HOT DOG.
SAY: **I'D** LIKE A HOT DOG, PLEASE.
SAY: **I'LL** HAVE A HOT DOG, PLEASE.

DON'T SAY: I WANT TO SEE THIS BOOK!
SAY: **MAY I** PLEASE SEE THAT BOOK?

DON'T SAY: PLEASE GIVE ME THAT BOOK.
SAY: **MAY I** HAVE THAT BOOK, PLEASE?

DON'T SAY: I NEED SOME HELP, PLEASE!
SAY: **WOULD YOU MIND** GIVING ME A HAND?
SAY: **COULD YOU** LEND ME A HAND, PLEASE?
SAY: **WOULD YOU BE SO KIND AS TO** HELP ME, PLEASE?

GET IT? TRY *WOULD YOU BE SO KIND AS TO...*
WITH GROWNUPS AND NOTICE THEIR REACTION.

WHAT'S NOT DIPLOMATIC

YOU KNOW THIS JOKE?

A LADY GIVES A KID BREAD AND BUTTER.
THE KID SAYS, *THANK YOU!*
THE LADY SAYS: *I LOVE IT WHEN I HEAR
A THANK YOU - SO NICE!*
THE KID SAYS: *IF YOU WANNA HEAR IT AGAIN,
PUT SOME JAM ON IT TOO!*

OOPS! ASKING FOR MORE
IF YOU HAVE RECEIVED
A GIFT IS NOT DIPLOMATIC!
IT'S JUST BAD MANNERS!

MAY I HAVE SOME JAM ON MY BUTTER, PLEASE?

IF SOMEONE GIVES YOU A TOY,
OR CANDY, OR ANY OTHER GIFT,
IT'S IMPORTANT TO SHOW THEM
THAT YOU LOVE THAT GIFT,
AND THAT YOU ARE GRATEFUL.
IF YOU IMMEDIATELY
ASK FOR MORE CANDY
OR ANOTHER TOY, THEY THINK
YOU DIDN'T REALLY LIKE
WHAT THEY GAVE YOU.
NOT GOOD!
YOU WANT THEM
TO ENJOY GIVING YOU GIFTS,
SO THEY'LL GIVE YOU
ANOTHER ONE NEXT TIME.

GET THEM TO LISTEN TO YOU.

DON'T SAY: CAN I SAY SOMETHING? OR CAN I TALK?
SAY: **MAY I PLEASE SAY SOMETHING?**

IF YOU ARE TALKING TO A FEW PEOPLE,
LIKE YOUR FAMILY, YOU CAN SAY
MAY I HAVE YOUR ATTENTION PLEASE?

DON'T SAY: WHAT? OR WHAT DID YOU SAY?
SAY: **PARDON ME?**
SAY: **SO SORRY, I DIDN'T QUITE CATCH THAT.**

IF GROWNUPS INTERRUPT YOU, SAY:
SORRY, COULD I JUST FINISH?

IF THEY DON'T UNDERSTAND YOU, SAY:
**PERHAPS I DIDN'T MAKE MYSELF CLEAR.
WHAT I WAS TRYING TO SAY WAS ...**

IF YOU SAID A WORD THAT GROWNUPS
FIND RUDE, APOLOGIZE LIKE A GROWNUP.
SAY:
**SORRY IT WAS A SLIP OF THE TONGUE.
PLEASE ACCEPT MY APOLOGY.**

IF YOU SAID SOMETHING THAT HURT ANOTHER PERSON,
NEVER SAY: I WAS JUST KIDDING
NEVER SAY: SORRY, BUT...
SAY: **I AM SO SORRY. I REGRET SAYING THIS.
PLEASE, FORGIVE ME.**

MAY I HAVE YOUR ATTENTION, PLEASE?

IF YOU DISAGREE...

DIPLOMATS NEVER USE STRONG NEGATIVE WORDS
LIKE *BAD* OR *WRONG*, BECAUSE THEY UPSET PEOPLE.
YOU NEED TO KEEP PEOPLE HAPPY IF YOU WANT THEM
TO AGREE WITH YOU. HERE IS WHAT TO SAY
IF YOU THINK SOMEONE IS WRONG.

DON'T SAY: YOU'RE WRONG.
SAY: I THINK YOU MIGHT BE MISTAKEN.
SAY: I'M AFRAID I DISAGREE.

DON'T SAY: THAT'S A BAD IDEA.
SAY: I'M NOT SO SURE THAT'S A GOOD IDEA.
SAY: I HAVE A FEW CONCERNS ABOUT THIS IDEA.
SAY: I DON'T THINK THAT'S SUCH A GOOD IDEA.

SOMETIMES IT'S BEST NOT TO DISAGREE AT ALL,
BUT INSTEAD JUST **EXPLAIN WHY THE PERSON'S IDEA
WON'T WORK.** YOU WILL SAY:

I SEE WHAT YOU MEAN, BUT...
(EXPLAIN WHY THEIR IDEA MAY NOT WORK).
I AGREE UP TO A POINT, BUT...

IF YOU DON'T LIKE SOMETHING

DON'T SAY: THIS LOOKS BAD.
SAY: **I THINK THIS NEEDS SOME IMPROVEMENT.**

DON'T SAY: I DON'T LIKE THIS.
SAY: **I'M NOT TOO FOND OF THIS.**
OR: **I'D PREFER A DIFFERENT WAY TO DO THIS.**

THIS IS HOW DIPLOMATS
MAKE PEOPLE LIKE THEM,
EVEN IF THEY DISAGREE!

*I THINK
THIS NEEDS SOME
IMPROVEMENT...*

THE LONGEST WORD IN ENGLISH

PNEUMONOULTRAMICROSCOPICSILICOVOLCANOCONIOSIS

IT HAS **45** CHARACTERS
IT'S A MEDICAL TERM USED BY DOCTORS TO DESCRIBE
A LUNG DISEASE THAT HAPPENS WHEN A VOLCANO
ERRUPTS FILLING THE AIR WITH SILICA DUST.
SILICA IS A MINERAL YOU FIND IN A LOT OF ROCKS.
A PERSON BREATHES IN THIS DUST AND GETS SICK.

SO THIS **45**-LETTER WORD IS MADE OF A FEW ROOTS
ALL COMING FROM LATIN. **THE ROOT OF A WORD** IS
ITS MAIN PORTION. FOR EXAMPLE, IF YOU TAKE
THE WORD *UNFINISHED* AND CHOP OFF THE PREFIX *UN-*
WHICH MEANS *NOT*, AND THE ENDING *-ED*,
YOU WILL HAVE THE ROOT OF THE WORD, *FINISH.*
LET US SEE HOW MANY ROOTS THE LONGEST WORD HAS

PNEUMONO-ULTRA-MICROSCOPIC-SILICO-VOLCANO-CONIOSIS

PNEUMONO = BREATHING, LUNGS
ULTRA = VERY
MICROSCOPIC = SMALL
SILICO = SILICA
VOLCANO = VOLCANO
CONIOSIS = DISEASE CAUSED BY DUST

WOW, DOCTORS ARE REAL HEROES,
NOT ONLY BECAUSE THEY SAVE LIVES,
BUT ALSO BECAUSE THEY HAVE
TO REMEMBER ALL THESE CRAZY LONG MEDICAL TERMS!!!

The Funniest Words

Here are some words
people think are funny...

Ragamuffin

Is a kid or a pet whose clothes
or fur is dirty! The word comes
from *rag* (piece of old fabric)
But why muffin?? Beats me!
For example, I can tell my son:
Please put on some nice clothes:
You can't go to a party looking like a ragamuffin!

Gobbledygook

Means nonsense, something that makes no sense
This word first appeared in American English
in the 1940s as an imitation of the sounds made
by a turkey: *gobble, gobble, gobble!*
Whatever turkeys are saying, it makes no sense
to us, so gobbledygook = nonsense.
For example, some babies think they can talk,
but actually they can't, they are just saying
some gobbledygook. You can't understand a word!

Precisely!

Gobbledygook, man!

DISCOMBOBULATED

BEFUDDLED

DISCOMBOBULATE

THIS WORD MEANS *TO CONFUSE SOMEONE* AS IN:
ALL THIS GOBBLEDYGOOK DISCOMBOBULATED ME!
OR *YOU LOOK DISCOMBOBULATED!*
THIS IS ANOTHER MADE-UP WORD:
SOMEONE IN THE **19**TH CENTURY THOUGHT
IT SOUNDED FUNNY AND WAS PERFECT
TO DESCRIBE THE STATE OF CONFUSION.

BEFUDDLE = DISCOMBOBULATE!

NO KIDDING, ANOTHER FUNNY WORD
THAT MEANS *TO CONFUSE SOMEONE!*

CURMUDGEON

(KAR-MAH-JUN) DO YOU KNOW
A KID WHO IS ALWAYS GRUMPY
AND COMPLAINING?
THAT'S A CURMUDGEON!

SOFT WORDS

OK, BACK TO THE DIPLOMATIC TALK!

SOMETIMES YOU JUST HAVE
TO SAY THINGS VERY DIRECTLY.
IN THAT CASE DIPLOMATS USE
WORDS THAT SOFTEN
WHAT THEY SAY,
THE SOFT WORDS, SUCH AS:
I AM AFRAID, A LITTLE BIT,
A LITTLE, A BIT, REALLY,
SLIGHT, SLIGHTLY, SMALL, ONE OR TWO.

Soft !

DON'T SAY: I DON'T LIKE IT
SAY: I DON'T REALLY LIKE IT, I'M AFRAID
DON'T SAY: YOU UPSET ME!
SAY: I AM A LITTLE BIT DISAPPOINTED.

ANOTHER WAY TO MAKE YOUR SPEECH
SOFTER AND MORE DIPLOMATIC IS THIS:
INSTEAD OF ASKING DIRECTLY:
CAN WE GO TO THE PARK TODAY?
SAY: I WAS HOPING WE COULD GO
TO THE PARK TODAY.
OR I WAS THINKING WE COULD
GO TO THE PARK TODAY.

Little!

I AM
A LITTLE BIT
DISAPPOINTED...

DIPLOMATIC ADVICE

IF YOU WANT TO GIVE ADVICE TO SOMEONE, ESPECIALLY
TO A GROWNUP, INSTEAD OF SAYING
DON'T DO THIS, DO THAT! OR *NEVER DO THAT!*
USE THESE DIPLOMATIC WORDS:
YOU MIGHT CONSIDER DOING THIS INSTEAD...

OR USE QUESTIONS LIKE:
HAVE YOU THOUGHT OF DOING IT THIS WAY?
WOULD YOU CONSIDER DOING THIS INSTEAD?
WOULDN'T IT BE BETTER TO DO IT THIS WAY?

IF YOU ARE DIPLOMATIC,
GROWNUPS WILL ALWAYS LISTEN TO YOU,
AND THIS IS HALF THE BATTLE WON:
YOU WANT THEM TO HEAR WHAT YOU SAY
AND TO TAKE IT SERIOUSLY.

BEING **DEFENSIVE**

IF YOU TELL SOMEONE: *YOU DON'T UNDERSTAND ME,*
IT SOUNDS LIKE YOU ARE ACCUSING THEM, POINTING
A FINGER AT THEM. PEOPLE MAY GET UPSET AT THAT
AND GET **DEFENSIVE.**
WHAT IS *DEFENSIVE*? THAT'S **WHEN A PERSON THINKS
YOU DISAPPROVE OF THEM AND START DEFENDING
THEIR IDEAS OR BEHAVIOR IN AN UPSET WAY.**
THEY CAN POINT THE FINGER AT YOU IN RETURN,
OR SAY SOMETHING MEAN, OR SCREAM, OR EVEN CRY.
DIPLOMATS MAKE SURE THEY NEVER MAKE ANYONE FEEL
DEFENSIVE. THEY TRY NOT TO USE THE WORD **YOU.**
INSTEAD THEY SAY **I.**

DON'T SAY: YOU DON'T UNDERSTAND ME.
SAY: **PERHAPS I'M NOT MAKING MYSELF CLEAR.**

DON'T SAY: YOU DIDN'T TELL ME THAT!
SAY: **I AM AFRAID I DON'T REMEMBER YOUR TELLING ME THAT.**

DON'T SAY: YOU DIDN'T EXPLAIN THIS TO ME!
SAY: **SORRY, I DIDN'T UNDERSTAND THIS POINT.**

DON'T SAY: YOU SHOULD HELP ME!
SAY: **I AM LOOKING FOR SOME HELP HERE.**

DON'T SAY: YOU BROKE MY TOY!
SAY: **MY TOY IS BROKEN.**

I AM LOOKING FOR SOME HELP HERE...

DON'T SAY: YOU PROMISED WE WOULD DO THIS TOGETHER!
SAY: **IT WAS AGREED THAT WE WOULD DO THIS TOGETHER.**

EUPHEMISMS

THAT RAT LEFT A LOT TO BE DESIRED...

EUPHEMISMS (YOU-FE-MISMS) ARE POLITE WORDS PEOPLE USE INSTEAD OF SAYING SOMETHING THAT MIGHT UPSET OTHERS. DIPLOMATS LOVE EUPHEMISMS AND USE THEM ALL THE TIME!

FOR EXAMPLE, TALKING ABOUT OLD PEOPLE A DIPLOMAT WOULD CALL THEM **OLDER** PEOPLE. NOT *OLD*! **NOBODY LIKES BEING CALLED** *OLD*!

ANOTHER EXAMPLE OF A EUPHEMISM IS **PASSED AWAY** INSTEAD OF **DIED**. IT'S **MORE RESPECTFUL**, ESPECIALLY IF YOU ARE TALKING ABOUT YOUR OR YOUR FRIENDS' FAMILY MEMBERS.

IF A DIPLOMAT TALKS ABOUT SOMETHING REALLY BAD, LIKE A BAD MEAL AT A RESTAURANT, THEY WILL USE A EUPHEMISM LIKE: **THAT HAMBURGER LEFT A LOT TO BE DESIRED.** IT'S LIKE SAYING, *I WISH IT WERE BETTER* INSTEAD OF *IT WAS JUST HORRIBLE*.

WHEN A DIPLOMAT IS TALKING ABOUT SOMEONE THEY THINK IS STUPID, THEY WILL NEVER SAY *STUPID*, INSTEAD THEY WILL SAY: **THAT GUY IS NOT THE SHARPEST PENCIL IN THE BOX.**

AND IF THEY SEE A FAT CAT, A DIPLOMAT WILL NEVER CALL IT *FAT*, BUT SAY

THAT CAT HAS A FEW EXTRA POUNDS!

DIPLOMATIC YES AND NO

If I ask you a favor (to do something for me), you will probably respond with *Yes* or *No*. Or you can say *Sure, No problem*, or *I can't*. Diplomats say these things in a different way. They say it diplomatically!

Instead of a simple *yes*, they will say: I'd be happy to help you. It would be my pleasure. And instead of *No, I can't*, they will say: I'm afraid I can't. Unfortunately, I'm not able to help you. Regrettably, I can't help you.

Words like **unfortunately** or **regrettably** signal that you wish you could help, but you really can't.

Diplomats behave diplomatically to make sure that people always listen to them and take what they say seriously. If you learn and use diplomatic language, you will make your friends and the grownups in your life respect you and listen to your every word.

PROFESSORS' ENGLISH

PROFESSORS TEACH AT UNIVERSITIES AND THERE ARE NOT MANY UNIVERSITY JOBS. YOU HAVE TO BE A *SMART COOKIE* TO GET ONE. TO SOUND IMPORTANT PROFESSORS USE LANGUAGE FULL OF BIG NORMAN CONQUEST WORDS, AND OFTEN USE LATIN OR FRENCH EXPRESSIONS.

AN EXPRESSION IS A FEW WORDS OFTEN USED TOGETHER. FOR EXAMPLE, COOKIE IS A WORD, BUT SMART COOKIE IS AN EXPRESSION; KIND IS A WORD, BUT WOULD YOU BE SO KIND... IS AN EXPRESSION.

PROFESSOR LOOKING IMPORTANT

IT TAKES A LOT OF YEARS AND HARD WORK TO GAIN ENOUGH KNOWLEDGE TO BE A PROFESSOR. BUT **TO TALK LIKE A PROFESSOR IS EASY!**

PROFESSORS WANT TO SOUND SMART, AND SO SHOULD YOU. LET'S LEARN SOME OF THEIR FAVORITE EXPRESSIONS, AND TRY TO USE THEM HERE AND THERE, ESPECIALLY WHEN YOU WANT GROWNUPS TO LISTEN TO YOU. TRUST ME, WHEN THEY HEAR YOU SAY **MAY I HAVE CARTE BLANCHE AT THE TOY STORE?** THEY WILL BE ALL EARS. CARTE BLANCHE (KART BLANSH) IS FRENCH FOR *WHITE CARD,* OR *A DOCUMENT THAT HAS NOTHING WRITTEN ON IT.* TO HAVE A CARTE BLANCHE MEANS PERMISSION TO DO ANYTHING YOU WANT! HAHA!

BIG WORDS: GOOD THINGS

GOOD OLD FRENCH-LATIN WORDS ARE PROFESSORS'
FAVORITES. HERE ARE SOME WORDS AND HOW TO USE THEM.

*I APPRECIATE
A GOOD DINNER.*

APPRECIATE
= BEING THANKFUL OR GRATEFUL FOR SOMETHING
I APPRECIATE IT = I AM GRATEFUL FOR IT

APOLOGIZE
= BEING SORRY
I APOLOGIZE = I AM SORRY

*I APOLOGIZE.
I DIDN'T MEAN
TO SWALLOW
THE PRINCESS.*

SPECTACULAR = GREAT, BEAUTIFUL
SHE WORE A SPECTACULAR COSTUME.
IT'S A SPECTACULAR IDEA.

GENEROUS = GIVING A LOT
HE IS A GENEROUS MAN.
*THANK YOU FOR YOUR
GENEROUS GIFT - I LOVE IT!*

EPIC = HUGE OR GREAT *THAT PARTY WAS EPIC.*

SOPHISTICATED = COMPLEX AND FANCY
IT'S A SOPHISTICATED PLAY SET.
THIS GAME IS SOPHISTICATED.
PROFESSORS LOVE SOPHISTICATED WORDS.

BIG WORDS: BAD THINGS

OBNOXIOUS (OB-NOK-SHUS) = BAD BEHAVIOR
USE THIS WORD TO DESCRIBE KIDS
WHO DON'T LISTEN TO THEIR PARENTS
OR TEACHERS, AND DON'T PLAY FAIR
WITH OTHER KIDS.
SHE IS OBNOXIOUS.
I DON'T WANT TO BE FRIENDS WITH HER.

VICIOUS (VEE-SHUS)
= EVIL AND MEAN
HER WORDS WERE VICIOUS.

EMBARRASSING
= SOMETHING THAT MAKES
YOU FEEL SHAME
I FORGOT THIS GIRL'S
NAME: IT WAS EMBARRASSING!

OMINOUS
= DARK AND SCARY
THE SKY LOOKS OMINOUS,
THE STORM IS COMING!

TANTRUM = CRYING
AND SCREAMING ANGRILY.
BABIES HAVE TANTRUMS
IF THEY ARE HUNGRY.

I'LL GET YOU!
I'LL TELL
YOUR PARENTS!

BIG WORDS: STRANGE THINGS

HILARIOUS = FUNNY

RIDICULOUS = NO GOOD AND FUNNY
Do I look ridiculous in this hat?
This kid comes up with the most ridiculous ideas!

ABSURD = MAKES NO SENSE
This plan is absurd.

PREPOSTEROUS
= ABSURD AND RIDICULOUS!
That's a preposterous suggestion.

> *YOU MISINTERPRETED MY WORDS!*

> *WHAT DO YOU MEAN I LOOK RIDICULOUS IN THIS HAT??*

UNDERSTANDING

TO ELABORATE = TO EXPLAIN
I have a brilliant plan.
Let me elaborate.

MISINTERPRET = MISUNDERSTAND
You misinterpreted my words:
I didn't mean to upset you.

ABSOLUTELY = SURE
USE THIS WORD INSTEAD OF *SURE*
WHEN YOU AGREE TO DO SOMETHING.
IF THEY ASK YOU:
CLEAN UP YOUR ROOM!
RESPOND WITH *ABSOLUTELY!*

AM I HUNGRY? ABSOLUTELY!

INCLINED = PREFER
*WOULD YOU LIKE TO GO TO THE PLAYGROUND
OR A TOY STORE? I AM INCLINED TO GO TO THE TOY STORE.*

UNILATERAL DECISION = A DECISION
MADE WITHOUT ASKING OTHER PEOPLE'S OPINION.
*SHE MADE A UNILATERAL DECISION
TO STOP PLAYING WITH US.*

ADAMANT = WON'T CHANGE THEIR MIND
HE'S ADAMANT THAT HE IS NOT COMING WITH US.

REASONABLE = HAVING GOOD JUDGEMENT,
GOOD IDEAS
*YOU ARE NOT BEING REASONABLE,
YOU'RE DEMANDING THINGS THAT ARE IMPOSSIBLE*

YOU ARE NOT BEING REASONABLE!

IDIOMS (1)

Hold your horses!
I am **exhausted** (= tired)!
Too many big words!
I am taking a unilateral
decision to take a break.
Let's talk about something fun,
like the funniest expressions
we know... How about:

Cool as a cucumber
= calm
Hold your horses!
= wait a moment!

A storm in a teacup
= when someone makes
a big fuss about something
ridiculously small, as in:
Why is she screaming?
Nothing serious, a storm in a teacup!

These expressions are called **IDIOMS**.
An idiom is an expression whose meaning doesn't
equal the meaning of the words that make it.
Storm in a teacup doesn't mean that
there is bad weather in your teacup.

There are lots of idioms
in every language,
and some of them are hilarious!

IDIOMS (2)

BENT OUT OF SHAPE
= UPSET

WHY ARE YOU SO BENT OUT OF SHAPE?

I CAN'T WRAP MY HEAD AROUND THIS!
= I DON'T UNDERSTAND THIS!

DON'T BEAT AROUND THE BUSH!
= JUST SAY WHAT YOU REALLY MEAN!

CAUGHT RED-HANDED
= WHEN SOMEONE SAW YOU DOING SOMETHING BAD
SHE WAS EATING MY COOKIES! I CAUGHT HER RED-HANDED!

BARKING UP THE WRONG TREE
= TO BE MISTAKEN ABOUT A SITUATION, AS IN:

MY BROTHER SAYS I ATE HIS COOKIES. HE IS BARKING UP THE WRONG TREE!

WOOF! WOOF! WOOF!

FRENCH WORDS AND EXPRESSIONS

MANY WORDS USED BY PROFESSORS COME FROM OTHER LANGUAGES. KNOWING FOREIGN LANGUAGES IS A MUST FOR ANY PROFESSOR, AND SO THEY END UP USING A LOT OF WORDS FROM FRENCH, LATIN, OR OTHER LANGUAGES. HERE ARE A FEW FRENCH WORDS YOU CAN USE TO IMPRESS GROWNUPS AT HOME AND AT SCHOOL.

CARTE BLANCHE (KART BLANSH)

PERMISSION TO DO ANYTHING YOU WANT.
I CAN STAY HOME, OR PLAY OUTSIDE, OR GO ON A PLAY DATE - MY MOM GAVE ME CARTE BLANCHE.

DILETTANTE (DEE-LE-TANT)

A PERSON WHO THINKS THEY ARE AN EXPERT AT SOMETHING, BUT ACTUALLY THEY ARE NOT.
HE SAYS HE IS A PAINTER, BUT ACTUALLY HE IS JUST A DILETTANTE.

TETE-A-TETE (TET-AH-TET)

A MEETING BETWEEN TWO PEOPLE.
TETE IN FRENCH MEANS A HEAD.
SO TETE-A-TETE = HEAD-TO-HEAD
CAN WE HAVE A TETE-A-TETE TO DISCUSS MY BIRTHDAY PARTY?

FAUX PAS (FO-PAH) MEANS WRONG STEP IN FRENCH.

SOMETIMES YOU MAKE A SILLY MISTAKE THAT MAKES YOU FEEL EMBARRASSED, ASHAMED - IT'S A FAUX PAS.
I MADE A TERRIBLE FAUX PAS - I CALLED SUZY BETTY BY MISTAKE!

LATIN WORDS AND EXPRESSIONS 1

QUID PRO QUO (KWID PRO KWO) - THIS FOR THAT.
YOU DO SOMETHING FOR SOMEONE, AND THEY
DO SOMETHING FOR YOU.
*IT WAS A QUID PRO QUO: I WASHED THE DISHES,
AND MY MOM LET ME WATCH TV.*
*LET ME HELP YOU: IT'S NOT A QUID PRO QUO,
I DON'T WANT ANYTHING IN RETURN.*

INTER ALIA (INTER AY-LEE-AH)
IN LATIN MEANS AMONG OTHER THINGS.
*I WAS DOING MY HOMEWORK, AND
INTER ALIA WRITING CHRISTMAS CARDS.*

AD NAUSEAM (ADD NAW-ZEE-UM)
WHEN SOMETHING IS REPEATED OVER
AND OVER AGAIN UNTIL YOU'RE SICK OF IT.
AD NAUSEAM IN LATIN MEANS - UNTIL YOU ARE SICK.
*I AM SO TIRED OF HIM TELLING EVERYONE ABOUT HIS TRIP
TO DISNEYLAND AD NAUSEAM.*

AD INFINITUM (ADD IN-FIN-NITE-TUM) - ENDLESSLY,
ALL THE TIME. *AD INFINITUM* IN LATIN MEANS -
INTO INFINITY, WITHOUT END.

ET CETERA (ET SET-TER-RAH) - *AND SO ON* IN LATIN.
*I WAS DOING MY HOMEWORK, WRITING
CHRISTMAS CARDS, FINISHING MY LEGO
PROJECT, ET CETERA.*
ET CETERA IS OFTEN WRITTEN IN A SHORT FORM: ETC.
FOR EXAMPLE, *I PACKED MY CLOTHES, MY TOYS,
MY BOOKS, ETC.*

LATIN WORDS AND EXPRESSIONS 2

MEA CULPA (MAY-AH KOOL-PAH)

IS *MY BAD*, OR *MY FAULT* IN LATIN.
YOU SAY IT WHEN YOU APOLOGIZE.
*I AM SO SORRY I DID THIS, IT WAS
A MISTAKE - MEA CULPA!*

> *MEA CULPA!
> I DIDN'T MEAN
> TO SWALLOW
> YOUR CAT!*

MODUS OPERANDI (MOH-DOOS OH-PEHRANDI)

THE WAY SOMEONE PREFERS TO DO THINGS.
*A SQUIRREL HIDES IN THE TREE, AND WHEN YOU LEAVE, IT
STEALS NUTS FROM THE TABLE - THIS IS ITS MODUS OPERANDI.*

PERSONA NON GRATA

(PERSO-NAH NON GRAH-TAH) AN UNWELCOME PERSON
*THIS GIRL IS OBNOXIOUS: SHE IS PERSONA
NON GRATA IN OUR HOUSE.*

STATUS QUO (STAH-TUS KWO) SITUATION AS IT IS.

PARKS CLOSE AT DARK - THAT'S THE STATUS QUO.

SOME ITALIAN WORDS ARE ALSO OFTEN
USED BY PROFESSORS, FOR EXAMPLE:

FIASCO - A PLAN THAT GOES WRONG

USE IT ANY TIME YOU TALK ABOUT A BIG DISASTER.

BIZZARRE = VERY STRANGE AND UNEXPECTED

*HER BEHAVIOR IS BIZZARRE: WHAT'S WRONG
WITH HER?*

STRATEGY: GETTING TO YES

OK, IT'S TIME TO PUT TOGETHER ALL THE INFORMATION
WE HAVE GATHERED ABOUT TALKING TO GROWNUPS AND
COME UP WITH A WINNING STRATEGY TO GET A **YES**
TO ANY REASONABLE REQUEST YOU HAVE.

TRY TO BE DIPLOMATIC AND SUPER POLITE EVERY DAY
TO TEACH THE GROWNUPS AROUND YOU TO LISTEN TO YOU.
YOU WANT TO SHOW THEM THAT YOU DESERVE THEIR TRUST.

DON'T TALK TO THEM WHEN THEY'RE IN A BAD MOOD
OR IN THE MIDDLE OF DOING SOMETHING ELSE.
WAIT UNTIL THEY ARE RELAXED AND HAPPY.

WHEN YOU ARE READY TO TALK TO THEM,
MAKE EYE CONTACT WITH THEM, THAT IS
LOOK THEM IN THE EYE. MAKE SURE YOUR
VOICE IS CALM, NOT UPSET, NOT WHINY.

ASK THEM FOR THEIR ATTENTION POLITELY:
CAN YOU SPARE A MOMENT TO TALK WITH ME?
I'D LIKE TO ASK YOU SOMETHING.

SOMETIMES YOU WANT TO ASK FOR SOMETHING YOU KNOW
YOUR PARENTS DON'T ALLOW. BUT MAYBE OTHER
PARENTS ALLOW THIS THING, SO YOU WANT TO TRY.
HERE IS WHAT YOU SAY:
MOM/DAD, I KNOW YOU DON'T USUALLY LET ME DO THIS,
AND I UNDERSTAND AND APPRECIATE WHY. BUT IT WOULD
MEAN A LOT TO ME IF YOU WOULD CONSIDER LETTING ME
DO IT THIS ONE TIME.

ASKING FOR A FAVOR OR HELP

A FAVOR IS A SMALL THING YOU DO TO HELP SOMEONE.
IF YOU ARE WORKING ON A SCHOOL PROJECT AND YOU NEED
SOME GROWNUP HELP OR TOOLS, ASK THEM FOR A FAVOR
FIRST, AND THEN TELL THEM WHAT HELP YOU NEED.

SAY: WOULD YOU DO ME A FAVOR? I NEED SOME HELP
FINISHING MY PROJECT.
COULD YOU POSSIBLY FIND SOME TIME TO HELP ME?
COULD I BOTHER YOU TO GIVE ME A HAND WITH
MY SCHOOL PROJECT?
COULD I TROUBLE YOU TO HELP ME WITH
MY SCHOOL PROJECT?
WOULD YOU MIND HELPING ME WITH MY PROJECT?
WOULD IT BE TOO MUCH TROUBLE FOR YOU TO HELP ME
WITH MY SCHOOL PROJECT?
BY ANY CHANCE COULD YOU HELP ME WITH
MY SCHOOL PROJECT?

EXPERTS SAY THAT IF YOU MAKE A REQUEST,
AND IMMEDIATELY TELL THE OTHER PERSON
THEY HAVE A CHOICE, IT'S MORE LIKELY THAT
THEY WILL SAY YES. SO ONCE YOU HAVE MADE
YOUR REQUEST FOR HELP OR FAVOR, SAY:

IF YOU CAN'T HELP OUT, I COMPLETELY UNDERSTAND,
BUT I THOUGHT I'D ASK.
I COMPLETELY UNDERSTAND IF YOU CAN'T; I KNOW
YOU ARE BUSY.
...BUT IF YOU CAN'T HELP ME FOR ANY REASON
THAT'S OKAY, I UNDERSTAND.

ASKING FOR THINGS OR FUN ACTIVITIES

IF YOU ARE ASKING A GROWNUP FOR THINGS OR FUN ACTIVITIES LIKE MOVIES, YOUR REQUEST WILL HAVE **3** PARTS:

1. GIVE A REASON FOR YOUR REQUEST
2. MAKE YOUR REQUEST IN A DIPLOMATIC WAY
3. GIVE THEM THE CHOICE OF SAYING **NO**
YOU KNOW THAT THIS CHOICE MAKES IT MORE LIKELY THAT THEY WILL SAY:

YES

EXAMPLE 1:
REASON FOR REQUEST:
MY FRIENDS ARE ALL TALKING ABOUT THIS NEW MOVIE...
REQUEST:
I THOUGHT I WOULD ASK YOU IF BY ANY CHANCE WE COULD GO SEE IT THIS WEEKEND...
GIVE THEM THE CHOICE:
I CERTAINLY UNDERSTAND IF IT'S NOT POSSIBLE FOR SOME REASON, BUT

I THOUGHT I'D ASK...

EXAMPLE 2:
REASON FOR REQUEST:
I WOULD LOVE TO TRY THIS NEW CONSTRUCTION TOY...
REQUEST:
I THOUGHT I WOULD ASK YOU IF BY ANY CHANCE I COULD REQUEST IT FOR MY BIRTHDAY/CHRISTMAS
GIVE THEM THE CHOICE:
I CERTAINLY UNDERSTAND IF IT'S TOO EXPENSIVE, BUT I THOUGHT I'D ASK.

KEEP YOUR PROMISE

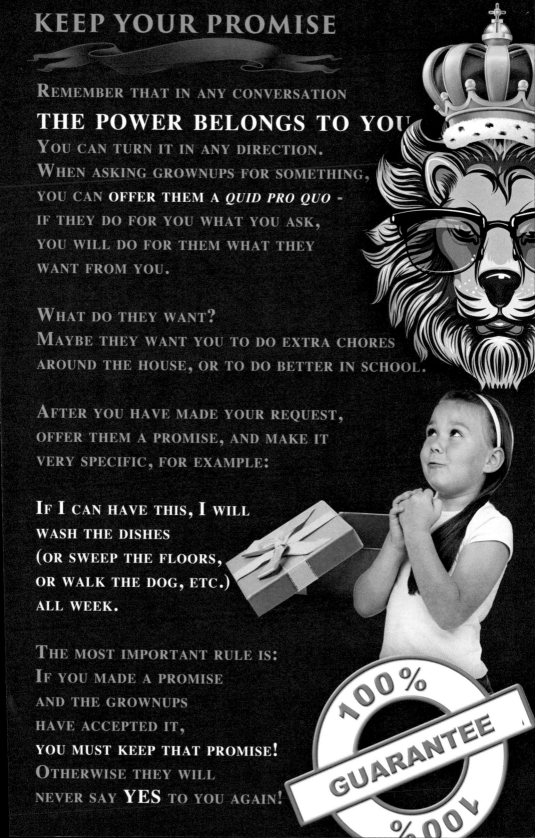

REMEMBER THAT IN ANY CONVERSATION

THE POWER BELONGS TO YOU

YOU CAN TURN IT IN ANY DIRECTION.
WHEN ASKING GROWNUPS FOR SOMETHING,
YOU CAN **OFFER THEM A** *QUID PRO QUO* -
IF THEY DO FOR YOU WHAT YOU ASK,
YOU WILL DO FOR THEM WHAT THEY
WANT FROM YOU.

WHAT DO THEY WANT?
MAYBE THEY WANT YOU TO DO EXTRA CHORES
AROUND THE HOUSE, OR TO DO BETTER IN SCHOOL.

AFTER YOU HAVE MADE YOUR REQUEST,
OFFER THEM A PROMISE, AND MAKE IT
VERY SPECIFIC, FOR EXAMPLE:

IF I CAN HAVE THIS, I WILL
WASH THE DISHES
(OR SWEEP THE FLOORS,
OR WALK THE DOG, ETC.)
ALL WEEK.

THE MOST IMPORTANT RULE IS:
IF YOU MADE A PROMISE
AND THE GROWNUPS
HAVE ACCEPTED IT,
YOU MUST KEEP THAT PROMISE!
OTHERWISE THEY WILL
NEVER SAY YES TO YOU AGAIN!

100%
GUARANTEE
100%

WHAT IF IT'S A NO

IF YOUR REQUEST IS TURNED DOWN,
DON'T GIVE UP YET.
ASK THE GROWNUPS
WHY THEY SAID NO TO YOU.
ONCE YOU KNOW THE REASONS,
TRY TO ARGUE WITH THOSE REASONS.
IMPORTANT:
YOU ARE NOT ARGUING WITH THE GROWNUPS,
BUT ONLY WITH THEIR REASONS. YOU CAN'T GET ANGRY,
AND YOU HAVE TO BE QUICK.
FOR EXAMPLE, IF THEY SAY,
YOU NEED TO BE OLDER TO WATCH THIS MOVIE
YOU CAN SAY:
IT CAN HELP ME LEARN TO BE MORE GROWNUP,
OR OTHER KIDS IN MY CLASS HAVE SEEN IT.

IF YOUR PARENTS SAY *NO* AGAIN,
DON'T ARGUE ANY FURTHER.
YOU DID YOUR BEST AND IT JUST
DIDN'T WORK OUT.
IF YOU THROW A TANTRUM, THE GROWNUPS
WON'T LISTEN TO YOUR REQUEST NEXT TIME,
THEY WILL EXPECT ANOTHER TANTRUM.

IF YOU GET A *YES* TO YOUR REQUEST, REMEMBER
TO THANK THE GROWNUPS. THANK THEM 2 TIMES:
1. AFTER THEY SAY YES,
2. AFTER YOU GET WHAT YOU ASKED FOR.
EVEN BETTER IF YOU CAN MAKE A THANK YOU CARD
FOR THEM, OR COME UP WITH A SMALL THANK YOU GIFT.